Poems

Barbara Irvin

Published by Barbara Irvin, 2024.

POEMS

First edition. September 11, 2024.

ISBN: 979-8227647948

Written by Barbara Irvin.

About These Poems

Anyone who thinks creating short poems isn't challenging is wrong. I had this perception until recently. Sometimes the words just fail to come. When rhyming is involved, the difficulty is even greater. Still, if one writes a couple of verses every day, one will eventually have enough to fill a collection.
Most of the poetry contained in this volume was written within a matter of days. My creativity must have been soaring. For those of you who write as well, you might have a sudden urge to put pen to paper or fingers to keyboard. If you simply prefer reading, I hope you like what is on the pages that follow.

A Breathtaking View
She looks out the window every night.
The stars in the sky are so bright.
She likes to walk in the moonlight.
The shimmering glow is a spectacular sight.

A Storm
It begins to pour.
The wind is so strong I think it will blow down the door.
Everything becomes dark.
A dog starts to bark.
In the distance, I hear a pop.
If only this storm would stop.

Friendship
What is a friend?
Someone who is there until the end.
He or she supports you over the years.
You can lean on him or her when you need to shed tears.

At The Beach
The movement of the waves is a soothing sound.
People are all around.
Kids build castles in the sand.
Couples walk hand in hand.

A World Of Possibilities

Seeing is believing is what they say.

You can accomplish a goal on any given day.

Why is this sometimes hard?

A dream is as precious as a postcard.

After The Storm
They stare at a pastel rainbow.
It is as beautiful as freshly fallen snow.
The sky was gray.
Now, the sun is out, and it is a perfect day.
Children want to play.

Learning
There are things everybody should know.
Kids need to thrive and grow.
Some have a huge desire to learn.
Those who do deserve a turn.
Anyone can educate.
The impact you make is great.

Nature Hike
I look at the beauty surrounding me.
The forest is exactly where I want to be.
Plants are nourished by the sun.
Walking through the woods is fun.

Nervous Bliss
A girl enters the cafe every day.
The boy who waits on her makes her feel a certain way.
She wants to talk to him outside of there, but does not know what to say.

A Thirst To Accomplish
People need goals to strive for.
When nothing happens, it can feel like there is a closed door.
One can have the world and still want more.
Ideas are meant to explore.

Outside Joy
Kids want to be outdoors all day.
They run and play.
A boy flies a kite.
The sun is shining bright.
By nightfall, he will be ready for bed.
The boy will go to sleep while images of the enjoyment he had float around in his head.

The Puppy
The puppy likes to yap.
He takes a nap.
His food is in a large bowl.
Children stop to admire him on their way to school.

A Butterfly
A butterfly flutters overhead.
It is yellow and red.
A butterfly is a symbol of love.
It is as pretty as a dove.

The Dance
A sign hangs on the wooden door.
People walk on the recently scrubbed gym floor.
There will be punch.
The food will be far better than what was served for lunch.

The Allure Of The Water
The water is cool.
It is like stepping into a pool.
Its trickling sound makes you want to get into a boat.
There is nothing more relaxing than lying on a raft while you float.

A Dancing Doll
I remember a particular doll.
I probably got her at some store in the mall.
I'd wind the doll up and watch her twirl.
As I recall, her hair had lots of curl.

The Cat
The cat has lots of fur.
She likes to purr.
Her favorite toy is a ball.
She washes her paw.

On The Ice
She slowly makes her way on the ice.
Her outfit is nice.
Like other skaters, she wants to glide.
However, her foot begins to slide.

A Tree

A tree starts out small.

Suddenly, it is very tall.

Its leaves change colors in the fall.

A caterpillar gets on the bark and likes to crawl.

Time
They watch the minutes creep by.
If only time would fly.
That happens when people have fun.
There is so much studying to be done.

Snow
Snow covers the ground.
It makes a crunching sound.
All around is a world of white.
It is a cold night.

On A Roll
You roll the dice.
Will your lucky number come up twice?
Is this some kind of sign?
For an instant, you feel as if you've drank a lot of wine.

The Art Of Writing
The words flow from his pen.
He writes in his den.
It is his favorite place to be.
When he writes, he feels totally free.

A Spring Day
Birds chirp in the trees.
The pollen in the air makes me sneeze.
I wish I had some oranges to squeeze.
I would enjoy a glass of juice in the warm breeze.

Memories Of Fun
An appetizing smell wafts through the air.
It reminds her of the fair.
That is where she got her first teddy bear.
How she longs to go back there!

The Glittering Gown
It is the glitziest gown I've ever seen.
The color is medium green.
I have to admire it from afar.
It will probably end up being purchased by some star.

The Toy
The little girl hugs her stuffed animal very tight.
It keeps her company throughout the night.
When the toy isn't beside her, nothing seems right.
It is as necessary as a light.

Putting Feelings On Paper
It's said a pen is as powerful as a sword.
Sometimes one must struggle to come up with an effective word.
Creativity flows like ink.
Writing requires one to think.

Going For A Run
They go for a run each day.
It is invigorating in every way.
Afterwards, they have an unquenchable thirst.
Sometimes they get caught in a cloudburst.

A Chef's Dream
She loved to cook.
Her recipes were organized in a notebook.
She liked the tartness of cherry.
It tasted far better than blackberry.

Sweltering
It is so hot.
An animal tries to find a shady spot.
Plants droop in a pot.
They are in desperate need of water, which is in the pitcher that was just bought.

The Fire
She stares into the fire.
It's easy for her to transpire.
The flames are bright.
She keeps warm on a chilly night.

The Trail

It was a long hike.

They passed someone on a bike.

There was a nearby dam.

The lunches they ate contained pieces of cheese and ham.

The Clown
There was a clown.
His shoes were brown.
He brought lots of cheer.
Boys and girls looked forward to the circus every year.

The Dog
The dog wants fed.
His ball is red.
He pushes it with his left paw.
It lands near the seesaw.

Eating A Tart
She bites into a tart.
It is shaped like a heart.
The outer layer is so moist it falls apart.

Nearby
A phone rings.
A bird sings.
People dance.
The day brings a new chance.
Someone goes for a walk.
Two people sit on a bench and talk.

A Winter Show
The audience waits for the conductor to cross the stage.
The piano player makes sure he has the correct page.
It will be a glorious show.
There will even be fake snow.

Taking A Walk
The hill is steep.
I hear a horn beep.
I find a coin to keep.
After strolling, I fall asleep.

In The Moment
I am wearing pink.
I need to think.
I imagine a coat made of mink.
I'm sipping a frozen drink.

The Panda Bear
The panda bear is worn.
Its bowtie is slightly torn.
Still, the bear is a special toy.
It continues to bring comfort to the little boy.

A Chocolatey Dream
The chocolate is as smooth as silk.
It is made with milk.
The center of the candy is creamy.
The feeling you get when you eat one is dreamy.

A Library

A library is a special place.
There is a lot of space.
Some books are rare.
People volunteer because they care.

Stories
Stories can inspire.
They can ignite an inner fire.
A reader might wish to write his or her own someday.
He or she will use experiences and research in a unique way.
Will the artistic endeavor be great?
It shall be determined by fate.

Mom
Thank you for all you do.
I know I don't say this enough, but these words are very true.
I love you.

Poetic Power
Poetry is truth.
It is popular among the youth.
Some poets recite.
They are at peace when they write.

Changing Seasons
I see leaves of red and gold.
This is a sign that the weather will soon be cold.
Bring out the winter attire.
Soon people will want to sit by a fire.

The Desire Within
I have an immense desire.
All I want is to inspire.
This is a huge need.
It is to succeed.

Baking A Cake
There is something I want to make.
I find a recipe for a cake.
It sounds like a baker's dream.
The frosting is buttercream.

At Play
She chases the ball everywhere.
It is way better than a stuffed bear.
Her friends throw it around.
They are at the playground.

The Top
I watch the top spin round and round.
It tips over on the ground.
I don't know where the top was found.
As it moves, it makes a funny sound.

At The Park
His mom takes him to the park.
He hears a dog bark.
His mom puts him on the swing.
The bluebirds sing.
It was a good day.
There will be more play.

The Ball
She bounces the ball.
It is not small.
She likes to watch it roll across the floor.
It lands by the door.

For A Father
"She'll always be Daddy's girl."
That's what they say.
She cherishes him, not just on Father's Day.
Sometimes they don't see eye to eye.
When that happens, she wants to cry.
Because of him, she will always try.

Outdoors
She gazes at the sky.
A baby bird attempts to fly.
She wishes she could climb a tree.
It seems like the ideal spot to be.

My Cat
My cat is sweet.
She likes to be neat.
My cat kisses my cheek.
Her meow is actually a squeak.

Summertime
I feel the sun on my back.
I hear the ducks quack.
I'm enjoying a delicious snack.

A Glass Of Tea
Tea soothes the soul.
I drank it after school.
I used lots of ice.
Some blends have a touch of spice.

The Flowers
The flowers are in bloom.
They can be seen from inside the room.
The flowers are blue.
She went into her garden and picked one especially for you.

A Family
She looks into his eyes.
Their newborn baby cries.
Their future has just begun.
They are now one.

A Dancer
A dancer works out on a mat.
Her tummy is flat.
She once was fat.
The dancer no longer reflects on that.

Ideas
Ideas are all around.
One is just waiting to be found.
You will know if it is right.
It will give you such delight.

Hunger
Something smells yummy.
I can feel the emptiness in my tummy.
I must eat.
I've waited hours for the marinated meat.

An Uncertain Possibility
You walk down the street.
You wonder who you might meet.
Could it be someone you previously ran into?
Maybe he or she will be somebody new.